Third Chance

Third Chance

Richard W. Turner, Sr.

COROIN BOOKS

For permission requests, contact books@coroin.com

Published by Coroin Books
https://coroin.com/books

ISBNs
eBook (EPUB): 978-1-963770-06-3
Paperback: 978-1-963770-07-0
Hardcover: 978-1-963770-08-7
LCCN (Library of Congress Control Number): 2025915961

Cover illustration by Carlos Maraver
https://vectorlance.com

CARPENTER OF NAZARETH
Copyright © 1999 by John Stafford and Richard W. Turner, Sr., recorded May 23, 1999.

EXPERIENCING DEUTERONOMY
Previously published by Richard W. Turner, Sr., distributed limited release December 27, 1998.

EXPERIENCING THE 139th PSALM
Previously published by Richard W. Turner, Sr., distributed in a limited release August 27, 1998.

This book is dedicated to
all those who were part of my "cocoon of prayer",
my friends who supported Caroline and me,
my family who were there for me,
physically, emotionally, and spiritually.
Special gratitude and love to my grandson, Erik Larson,
for his putting this work together.
Above all, to the love of my life, my wife, Caroline,
and to my God who gave me my Third Chance.

FOREWORD

A QUARTER-CENTURY HAS PASSED since we published the first edition of *Third Chance.* The day-to-day routines of life in the last years of the 20th century (before 9/11) seem so very different than the faster-paced, techno-centric, sound-bite and short-form narrative world of 2025.

In 1999, my mom asked me to help her get her dad's "book published", whatever that meant. He had a message to share with the world, she was his editor, and I signed up to help with the tech parts.

The Author, the Editor, and the Tech (Richard W. Turner, Sr., Sharyn T. Larson, and Erik R. Larson), 1999

My grandfather's words from 25+ years ago speak to me differently today, perhaps because I am double in age. Or maybe because I am now a father and grandfather. This second edition project has felt a bit "off" with both the Author (2004) and Editor (2025) having passed on.

The first edition cover design was hand-drawn by my grandfather, and as I recall, it cost extra to print the front cover in color.

Richard W. Turner, Sr. and Erik R. Larson, 2000

The deep roots and strong trunk of our family tree and the storytelling legacy continue, with another branch of father-daughter partnership having formed and bearing fruit.

The editing, formatting, and markup of the manuscript were done by Madailein Larson, who was born the year after her great-grandfather passed on. This second edition would not exist if not for her time and efforts. Thank you, Maddie <3

Changes from the first edition include punctuation, minor grammatical adjustments for readability, and an editorial change to the group the Bible studies together following the *Afterword*.

Shout out to the amazing and talented graphic designer Carlos Maraver (vectorlance.com) for the beautiful second edition cover design imagery, incorporating the original stained-glass motif and elements from the stories herein.

I am both honored and excited to bring the full catalog of my grandfather's works, including previously unpublished stories and verse, to a wider reach in the months ahead.

Erik R. Larson
Galveston, Texas
August 1, 2025

ACKNOWLEDGEMENTS

WITH THANKS

P RAYER BROUGHT ME BACK from the entrance to heaven.

The doctors must be acknowledged: Dr. James Jones, my primary physician, who brought in Dr. Clifford Abels, Dr. Stuart Garner, Dr. Gardiner Roddy, Dr. Chris Teigland, and many others. There were nurses, aids, physical therapists like Don, Sherry, Jennifer, and others. Surely, all of these people were being covered by prayer.

Our church, Carmel Presbyterian of Charlotte, NC, started weaving a "cocoon of prayer" from the time that my cancer was discovered. This family of Christians wrapped Caroline and me in their arms. Steve Cathcart, our minister, proved to be the true example of the word "pastor."

Many of our friends from back through our lives supported Caroline: among them, Bo and Lib Dyches from Aiken, SC, and those who have been part of our sharing group for almost thirty years, Bob and Nancy McDuffie, John and Peggy Garrett, and Mike and Mary Castano. Thanks also to Ouida Gregory, who became Caroline's "taxi service" when she was unable to drive because of her injury from a fall.

Prayers were offered by innumerable, unknown churches from New York to Florida to Texas and even as far away as Greece. We received over 200 cards of support. Unnumbered phone calls prompted Caroline to put a daily update on our answering machine, which addressed the concerns of callers. Our appreciation goes to those who sent flowers, gifts, and cards, brought food to our home, visited, and who made this experience tolerable.

Of course, my family, who kept in touch and visited during those long weeks, can never be thanked enough: from Columbus, OH, my brother Hank and his wife Laurene; from Pinellas Park, FL, my brother Roger and his wife Jean; and from Wilmington, NC, Caroline's brothers Carmer and his wife Pat, and Norman and his wife Rosalie.

Our daughter Sharyn flew in from Plano, TX, twice: once on a 15-minute notice and then again for my 74th birthday, which I celebrated March 14, 1998. Sharyn also suggested the comprehensive log, which was kept by anyone who spent time with me in the hospital. Our grandson Erik Larson from Plano, TX, put this narrative together on his computer and gave direction in editing and production.

Our daughter Nancy and her sons drove in from Aiken, SC, three times, once even at night. Her presence always brings a gentle touch. Of course, every time any of our children or grandchildren arrived in my room, it was like a shot in the arm. (These were good shots. No pun intended.)

Then there was our son Rick, and his wife Diane, from Ft. Mill, SC. I have no idea how many times they drove those 20 miles from their home to Charlotte. At least one of them was in my room just about every day. Thank you, Diane, for your ingenuity using a syringe and plastic tube to feed me mashed potatoes and milk when I was unable to eat regular food.

How proud I am of Rick. He is a good man. That is over-simplified and understated, but he is a modest man who is unselfish in his service to his family. Rick stayed many nights and was always there early each morning to meet the doctors and get their latest findings, usually before 7 am. He is the one who sensed the time to bring in other doctors to meet my needs at the lowest point of my illness.

In all humility, I cannot say enough about my love and appreciation for the support from our children's spouses and our grandchildren. By now, I have tried to express my thanks to a few of those who were so important to my recovery. But there is no way any of this could be possible without Caroline, the love of my life and my wife of 55 years.

Caroline slept on hospital cots every night during those first weeks. Then she had the flu and suffered injuries from a fall while I was in my most critical time. After her recovery, she came at least twice a day, every day, for the remainder of those eleven weeks. Caroline answered all those phone calls and inquiries, ran the household, and was my chauffeur during my weeks of therapy and for months after. She also typed the rough draft as I dictated this narrative.

She gave me her life, her support, and her love for over half a year, and she smiled every time I saw her. How can I express my thanks and love other than to say, "I love you, always."

Richard W. Turner, Sr.
Charlotte, NC
June 1999

CONTENTS

INTRODUCTION

L ET ME EXPLAIN THE title. Then you can continue to explore with me how I arrived at "Third Chance."

I believe in God. I have always believed in God, but He was kind of an umbrella, a shelter, and even a last resort at times.

As an umbrella, He seemed to provide a place where I could be safe from all the unknown problems of life. As a shelter, He was a place where I could go to get help when those unavoidable problems came into my life.

As a last resort, He was the One to whom I turned only when I reached "the bottom" in my struggle with what seemed to be insurmountable problems. Today, He is still my umbrella, still my shelter, and often still my last resort.

Three times in my life, I have had real spiritual experiences that seem to be miraculous enough that I should have seriously changed my life, to try to practice His presence in my everyday life, and this Third Chance *finally* awakened me.

When my Third Chance came, I thought it was God allowing me to return from the edge of Heaven so that I could tell my wife Caroline all the reasons I was about to go to see Jesus.

Now I have come to realize that was just part of the reason. Perhaps the biggest was to allow me time to learn humility and to share with others what my walk through this life has been about. Or perhaps, I am the reason He allowed me to return.

I have constantly asked the Holy Spirit to give me the words to share with you. If it appears that I am boasting or on an ego trip or am embellishing the truth in any way, please re-read that portion of this endeavor and do as I have done. Pray that the Lord will reveal why these words have been written.

As you may come to understand, I have not always been with God, but God has always been with me. Perhaps after you read this somewhat disjointed narrative, you will come to realize, as I think I finally have, that it takes whatever life we have to complete what God has planned for us.

If we will just seek forgiveness for our sins, ask Jesus to come into our hearts, and listen to His direction through the Holy Spirit, then we will have made the most important, faithful, truthful, and fruitful decision of our lives.

The following pages are not necessarily chronological. They tell of my walk through life, at times by myself, with my family, and with my many friends, slowly coming to the realization that I must first walk with God.

An Angel over the Himalayas

Woe to those who are wise in their own eyes, and clever in their own sight.

Isaiah 5:21

WHEN YOU ARE AT 15,000 feet in the Himalayas, you have other mountains in the area as high as 22,000 feet. If your airplane is loaded with bombs, drums of gasoline, food supplies for troops and service people, medical supplies, the list goes on and on, you need to know where you are at all times as you fly from India to China.

This was the situation I was in, along with another pilot and radio operator, flying a C-46 cargo plane from Mohanbari Air Base in India, headed for Kunming, China. It was 1945, and our missions were to supply everything needed for the war effort to drive out the Japanese. We were in the CBI Theater (China, Burma, India) during World War II, flying the original airlift over what we affectionately called The Hump (the Himalayas).

Our missions were combat-rated because the Japanese occasionally had planes in the air to intercept our unarmed and unescorted cargo planes. However, our biggest enemy was not the Japanese, but the flying conditions found over the Himalaya Mountains.

On this particular mission, we were flying on instruments because of a tremendous storm system. Back in 1945, we had no instrumentation to tell us where those huge storms were, so we just had to fly blind, day or night, hoping to get through as soon as possible.

This particular night, we were suddenly tossed about as we entered the storm. St. Elmo's Fire, a phenomenon caused when static electricity is generated by storm conditions, was framing our windshields and the leading edges of our wings and was creating circles on the tips of our propellers.

Then we ran into icing conditions. Ice formed on our wings and on the engine nacelles. The pneumatic de-icers on our airplane were long gone, due to the beatings they took from the weather. We realized we were losing altitude, which was a no-no in that part of the world.

Our radio operator made contact with an emergency airstrip in the Yunnan Province, and we picked up their radio beam. The idea was to "ride the beam" that is sent out from radio transmitters on the ground. These radio beams guided aircraft in a safe direction, provided the aircraft maintained enough altitude to clear any obstacles in its path.

The "beam" was a constant sound in the pilot's earphones. If he strayed to either side of the beam, he picked up either a dit-dah or a dah-dit. This was Morse Code for the letters A and N, respectively. The further from the transmitter, the broader the beam; the closer to the transmitter, the narrower the beam. This made flying or "bracketing the beam" more difficult as he came closer to the source of transmission.

Here we were, loaded with 55-gallon drums of gasoline bound for China, flying on instruments, "illuminated" with St. Elmo's Fire, unable to maintain altitude due to ice on our wings, and then we ran into hail! I had always thought of hail as ice particles about the size of marbles or even as big as golf balls. But this hail was the size of softballs! (No wonder our wings had dents in them!)

Fortunately, we were able to let down on our beam until we finally lost the ice and broke through the clouds a couple hundred feet above the approach to the runway. Those runway lights sure were welcome! It felt good to be on the ground, get some hot food, and a little rest until the morning brought an end to the storm.

The next morning, we prepared to take off, and I looked back at the approach we had made during the night. We had come down parallel to the side of a mountain on the left. On the right was a pagoda-type building 30 or so feet tall sitting on a small hill. We had flown the beam between a mountain and a pagoda with what seemed to be only a couple hundred feet on either side.

I thought I was the pilot of the airplane that night, and I don't think that I even thanked God at the time. But now I know that God had sent some fantastic angel to get us down on the ground.

A LITTLE BIT ABOUT MYSELF

M̲Y DAD, HENRY TURNER, my mother Ethel, my older brother Hank (HWT, Jr.), and I lived in a brown house on Sturdevant Street in the small village of Johnson City, NY.

This village was sandwiched between Binghamton and Endicott, in the Valley of Good Hope, at the junction of the Chenango and Susquehanna rivers. The three communities were separated by arches, over a common street that ran through all three towns. Johnson City was originally called Lestershire.

When George F. Johnson and Henry B. Endicott established the Endicott-Johnson Shoe Company in these towns, Johnson City became the headquarters.

My earliest memories go back to when I was about three years old. It must have been late winter because I remember standing on the edge of the street, wearing heavy clothes as the last snows were melting. In the 1920s, there were no street curbs, so when it rained or when the snow melted, the run-off made its way down the dirt streets.

There was a small twig shaped like a boat that was floating along the roadside waterway. It seemed to have a hard time navigating because it got stuck occasionally. I would lean over and nudge this adventurous twig-boat along its way. Perhaps because this "boat" had so much trouble and the water and air were so cold, it influenced me to never join the Navy.

About this time, Mother came home from the hospital. I did not know that she had been sick. But when I asked why she had gone to the hospital, there were vague replies. However, those little cries and whimpers just inside the French doors, which separated the living room from other parts of the house, made me a little suspicious.

Even at age three, there can be awareness of new joy when a baby (brother Roger) is brought home. New life is still a curiosity, more so now that I can look back 75 years and realize what God has done to create my own family.

Childhood and Teen Years

A T AGE FOUR OUR family moved to 101 Hill Avenue in Johnson City. Life was great: kindergarten at a tender age of five, watching the old steam rollers pave the dirt street with tar and gravel, chewing warm tar as a substitute for gum, playing mumbly-peg with a stick and a tapered peg of wood. How about cops and robbers? Or cowboys and Indians? Sandlot baseball? Some of the kids even had baseball gloves. Or what about marbles, tag, or hide-and-go-seek? I am so glad we did not have television during my childhood.

Saturdays, we went to the movies to see the next episode of *Tarzan and the Apes, Tom Mix, Zorro*, etc. On weekends, sometimes Dad made popcorn or the whole family joined in to churn homemade ice cream. In the summer, Mother showed us how to make root beer or birch beer and then cap the bottles. Driving to the country in our Model T Ford and later our Nash automobile to see Grandma and Grandpa Kreidler was fun.

In my pre-teen and early teen years, Dad and Mother put in a garden down near the river, with many other families. A plot of 20x60 feet yielded all kinds of good vegetables, many of which Mother canned and stored in the food cellar of the basement.

The family would go to the Grand Union grocery in our Model T Ford, and for about $15, we could fill the whole back part of the car. Mother would feed our family of five for two weeks on all that food.

Dad started as a mail boy at age 18 with the Endicott-Johnson shoe company and later became a pattern maker and designer for ladies' shoes. He was "highly paid" during the depression years with a salary of up to $22 a week. Yes, I do remember the depression of the early 30s, but we were fortunate to have a dad who set his goals, worked hard, and had a wife who knew how to make ends meet. Even if we kids had to put cardboard in our worn-out shoes to keep our feet warm and dry, Mother made us keep the tops of our shoes cleaned and polished.

My teen years were happy years. Because of Scouting, I spent a lot of time in the outdoors. Back then, you could get your driver's permit at age 16, your license at 18. In those days, we did not date until we approached 16. And my grades in school were in the top third, until I discovered girls.

I graduated in the January 1942 class at age 17. I wasn't at the top of the class, but I was the youngest graduate because I had enrolled in kindergarten in January, before I was five. So, my 13 years of school were from January 1929 to January 1942.

Perhaps because of the freedom and happiness of those childhood and teen years, I began to express myself creatively through woodcarving, sketching, and so forth. I was honored to have my design for the Johnson City High School class ring accepted and used for many years. This was part of my growing interest in creative hobbies that has extended throughout my life. Even then, God must have been at work.

BOY SCOUTS OF AMERICA

W HEN I WAS TWELVE years old, it was natural for me to do what many other boys did: join the Boy Scouts of America.

Just after I joined Troop 3 at Primitive Methodist Church, we went on an overnight campout. I remember two things, no three. First, we roasted marshmallows that night. Second, when I poked my head out of the pup tent in the morning, it was not only cold, but there were cows all around us. It was rather disconcerting at age 12 to awaken cold, hungry, and find cows in our campsite. Third, that was enough of the good ole BSA. I never went back to the meetings of Troop 3.

However, for some unknown reason, several months later, I joined Troop 105 at the Baptist church, about two miles from home. Mr. Cliff Springer was my Scoutmaster. In retrospect, Cliff did not look like Mr. Scoutmaster. But neither did we look like typical Norman Rockwell Boy Scouts in our makeshift uniforms, which were part official and part WWI hand-me-downs. We used old WWI backpacks, canteens, leggings, hats, and ammo belts mixed with khaki shorts and troop-designated neckerchiefs. I walked to meetings, regardless of the weather. That was what we did back in those days.

We camped on weekends at a church campsite about seven or eight miles north of town. Rain, shine, snow, or storms did not keep some of us from hiking out on Friday afternoons after school and returning either Saturday night or Sunday afternoon. This was a year-round activity. Besides, it qualified us for our required 14-mile hikes.

You learn a lot when you live outdoors in all kinds of weather. You learn how to build a fire in the rain, keep warm in the snow, and take time to dream about your future life as you lie in the meadow at night and study the stars.

I became an Eagle Scout on June 6, 1939. My ceremony was a meeting with some man in an upstairs room of the library in Johnson City. He gave me my badge and card, congratulated me, and we went our separate ways. A day or so later, a photographer from the Binghamton Press came to my home, sat me on the back-door steps, and took my picture for the paper. The poor man died either that day or the next, so my picture never appeared. However, there was a nice write-up. Not too many boys got their Eagle award back in those days.

This is all background for an experience that happened in 1973, 36 years later.

In 1959, I was employed by the BSA as a District Scout Executive. After assignments in Anderson, SC, Lakeland, FL, and Aiken, SC, I was assigned to a position in Charlotte, NC. We conducted roundtables for our adult scout leaders each month.

One Thursday evening in 1973, we had conducted our round-table at Mouzon Methodist Church. As we were cutting off the lights, a man appeared at the door and asked to see the minister. We told him that the minister was not in attendance. He walked away down the street, and we finished closing the building. For some reason, I felt I had failed this man. He may have had a very serious need, and I had not offered further help.

Mouzon Church is at the corner of Woodlawn Road and Selwyn Avenue. Woodlawn goes down a slight hill toward Sugar Creek. At that time, there was a steep embankment from the road down to a ravine and to the creek just below a bridge.

As I approached the bridge on my way home, I saw the man sitting on the side of the road facing the ravine. My little Volkswagen seemed to steer itself off to the right side of the road, and I parked. The man did not move when I crossed the street and asked him if he was all right. He appeared very despondent, and I was led to sit beside him. We talked. To this day, I have no idea what we said to each other, but it was evident that if we were to continue the conversation, we needed to move from where we were sitting, because the passing traffic was only a few feet from our backs.

We moved down the ravine a little way. We talked. The Lord must have been guiding my tongue because the man said that he did not need "this" anymore. "This" turned out to be a double-barreled shotgun, which he had kept from my view, hidden by a bush. He opened the action and out popped two shells.

We talked some more and went further down the ravine until we reached the creek bank. On the way down, he tossed the shotgun away and told me he had just escaped from prison. We talked some more, and all I remember was that we talked about the Lord and His forgiving love.

After talking for twenty or thirty minutes, suddenly a voice from the top of the ravine said that I should come up alone. Then I noticed that there were policemen surrounding us on the road, on the bridge, and on top of the ravine. They, of course, all had guns.

When I called back that the man was not armed, I heard the voice again. It was not a request; it was an order! "Come up now!" Well, under those circumstances, it seemed prudent to do as I was told.

After I climbed to the top of the ravine, I explained to the police why I was there. They saw my adult scout uniform and told me to get in my car and get out of there. I heard them say the man was an escaped convict from Asheville.

I tried to follow up on what happened to the man in the ravine, but I could never get any information. I did not even know the man's name.

Why do I tell you this story? Because I believe in angels. I am surely not an angel, ask anyone, but I believe God has angels in all kinds of places. Perhaps that night, there was not an angel available at that instant.

I believe I may have been used to keep that escaped convict from injuring someone or himself. Perhaps he needed someone with a listening ear, and maybe his ears were listening to what God needed him to hear. One thing I do know: God had another angel looking after me.

I know that I did not have anything to do with this event, but I believe God knew there would be a BSA roundtable that night and used these circumstances to help that man. I don't know if it helped him, but it certainly helped me realize the wonderful workings of God.

FIRST CHANCE

T RULY, THE FOLLOWING IS not the first time God tried to get my attention. But in my stubborn character, it is a very real and outstanding event that should have made me turn closer to my Father in heaven.

A little background: in November 1970, Mouzon Methodist Church had a Lay Witness Mission weekend. Caroline and I were on one of the committees, so naturally, I was exposed to this life-changing program. We always belonged to a church wherever we lived. I believed there was a God and knew the story of Jesus. I knew of Him but did not know Him personally. And I thought the Holy Ghost was some ethereal cloud floating somewhere in the rafters of the church. But that Saturday night of the mission program, I went to the altar and asked Jesus to let me get to know Him, to take away my false ways, and to forgive my sins.

Starting in January 1971, as a result of the Lay Mission, we organized our Sharing Group of five couples. We would meet weekly, become acquainted more intimately, learn more about the scriptures, and pray with and for each other.

Believe me, as we drove to that first sharing group meeting, I almost didn't make it. After all, share with these other people? Pray with them? Meet weekly, when I was already committed almost every night to some kind of BSA meeting? No way!

Caroline convinced me to give it a try. The Lord took over, and our lives were changed!

We met weekly, a miracle in itself, because every Thursday night came open or my BSA meetings were short enough for me to get to our sharing group.

We rotated meeting at each of our homes. The group grew at times to six or seven couples, but there were always four core couples. One evening in January 1972, we were at the home of Mike and Mary Castano. There were several other couples present that night, including a retired Episcopal priest named Father Sherry. After his retirement, he had received the Holy Spirit baptism, and he was really living for the Lord.

That evening Father Sherry told us of people who were healed of leg and back ailments when they had their legs lengthened, if one was shorter than the other. There was skepticism until Father Sherry put one of us in a chair, and at her request, he prayed for her leg to be lengthened. Her leg was lengthened, and she proclaimed her faith in God's healing power.

Back in 1962, I had been a passenger in a car accident when the door on my side was hit and smashed over me. A year later, the doctor operated and did a laminectomy on my fifth vertebrae. Ten days later, they sent me home, and for ten years, there was not a day that I did not have pain in my lower back. I was sure they had left a pair of scissors or other instruments in my back when they closed the incision! I was unaware of any difference in the length of my legs.

That night in 1972, I was persuaded to sit in a chair with Father Sherry kneeling in front of me, holding my feet in his hands and praying. We noticed before he prayed that my right leg was, indeed, about 1/2-3/4 inches shorter than the left.

Father Sherry prayed. My leg lengthened. Oh, how we praised the Lord! When I got home that night, I leaned over and touched my toes for the first time in ten years! Halleluia!

You would think I would have turned my old self around and done better. Well, I did for several months. At least I thought so. God must have thought I did not measure up, because more was yet to come. But He didn't give up. He never does.

A Long Courtship

I T WAS A PLEASANT evening that August 25, 1944. Lt. Ted Drust and Lt. Dick Turner were strolling down Front Street in Wilmington, NC, contemplating returning to Bluethenthal Air Base, where we were stationed. We were two pilots, serving our country in the United States Army Air Corps, waiting for the time we must go overseas and, if necessary, sacrifice ourselves to keep the world free from the tyranny of Adolf Hitler and the hordes of Japanese who had caused "a day that would live in infamy" at Pearl Harbor. Yes, we were two young daredevil hot pilots who would rid the skies of the enemy whenever we were called overseas.

In the meantime, our assignment at the Air Base was towing targets behind B-26s for fighter pilot trainees. We had earned our silver wings and gold bars just a couple of months before, so maybe we needed a little more experience. Sometimes we thought those students who shot at the targets needed more experience, too! Especially one student.

I was piloting a B-26 that was towing a target sleeve late one afternoon. An instructor and his student were to meet us for target practice. They were going to fly underneath the sleeve and then climb into a wing-over (which would reverse their direction and put them in position to fire at the target). Meanwhile, we proceeded straight and level.

However, the instructor's pattern was too tight, and he skimmed underneath our airplane instead of the sleeve. It was a rather uncomfortable near miss.

Then the student came in behind his instructor in his own P-47. Maybe his instructor had forgotten to tell him that his target was the sleeve and not our airplane. Anyhow, Mr. Student got to the top of his wing-over and lost airspeed. He headed straight for the mid-section of our airplane. Out of the corner of my eye, I happened to catch a glimpse of a huge engine and wings covered with white contrails, swooping down on us, out of control. It looked like an old-time steam locomotive coming out of a cloud.

Here we were, at 5,000 feet over the ocean, about three miles from the coast, in a medium bomber that was not supposed to fly like a fighter plane. If we got hit in the mid-section, where Mr. Student was heading, we had no chance to get out because all the hydraulics were in that section. We couldn't activate the bomb bay doors and jump, nor could we lower the nose wheel and go out the wheel well, unless we manually cranked the wheel down. The only way out would be through the cockpit overhead hatch. If we could get that hatch open, then the only obstacle was the huge rudder that looked like an oversized cleaver.

So, what to do? I hauled back on the yoke, jammed the throttles over the firewall, and banked to the right, putting that B-26 in an attitude that it was never built for. Now tell me, wasn't there an angel that lifted us out of harm's way?

We headed back to the airfield, cut loose the target, radioed in the reason why we cut the mission short, and suggested that Mr. Student needed to be taught a lesson. After landing, the student who tried to outsmart his instructor had to walk the tarmac that evening. We enjoyed watching his parachute slapping his legs every step of the way.

Back to that evening in August 1944: Suddenly, an automobile occupied by two pretty young ladies pulled up beside us and asked us if we needed a ride back to the base. Being very conscious of getting ensnared by femmes-fatales who may want to get vital wartime secrets from us to give to the enemy, but not wanting to offend the local citizenry who were a part of the nation we must defend, we had to give this great consideration. I am not sure who beat whom into the automobile with Nancy Crichton and her married cousin. Our consideration took at least two seconds.

To set the record straight, the people of Wilmington were very supportive of servicemen. It was their custom to offer rides and help, especially as gasoline was rationed and taxicabs were not too plentiful. It was a nice Southern gesture on their part.

Naturally, the married cousin would not date. But Ted asked Nancy for a date Saturday evening. She accepted and said she would try to get a date for me.

Ted and I met Nancy at 1705 Ann Street on Saturday, August 26, the home of my blind date. At first sight, I immediately fell in love with the 103-pound brunette dressed in her basic black dress and high heels. Her name was Caroline Elizabeth Davis. After dinner at the Officer's Club, the girls suggested we ride to Lumina, on Wrightsville Beach, a dance pavilion where the locals dated on Saturday nights. After returning to the base, I told Ted I was going to marry Caroline.

The next afternoon, Sunday, we all played golf, had dinner, and took in a movie. The theme song played was *Always* by Irving Berlin. This became "our song" for all the years that followed.

I didn't know then, but I do now, that God had provided me the love of my life. After calls on Monday and Tuesday night to Caroline, we dated Wednesday night and every night thereafter. For 55 years, I have been thanking God for Caroline!

After three weeks, I asked Caroline to marry me. She said we had not known each other long enough, so I waited 10 more days. On September 29, I gave her a diamond ring. She accepted.

On October 4, the Captain at the airbase heard of my serious intentions to get married, so he cut orders to ship me out the next week. He said these southern girls just wanted to marry pilots who would not survive the war, just to collect the $10,000 insurance! That was disgusting! I called the base commander named in my orders and explained my situation to him. He granted me a 10-day delay en route leave so we could get married.

On October 8, 1944, Caroline and I committed ourselves to each other in marriage. She and her mother, Myrtle, planned and accomplished a full church wedding and home reception for family and friends in just four days! Naturally, the organist played *Always* as we spoke our vows.

Caroline and I have learned the secret to an enduring marriage: we made a commitment before God to Him and to each other. We honor our commitment, *Always*.

Another angel must have arranged our blind date that night.

One Big Step

OUR MISSION WAS TO carry a load of bombs from India to Liuchow, China. Partway there, we were informed by radio that the runway had been bombed, but we could land on the taxi strip beside it. We were also told to be careful and, if the enemy appeared, to get out of the area quickly. The base would send us a warning.

It was a nice, clear day, and we could make out the jungles on the mountains and in the valleys below. It didn't look very inviting, and there were rumors that tribes of headhunters were down there. We were told to be sure to fasten our parachute harnesses if we had to jump. We heard that one pilot shot himself after his chute got caught in a tree. His chest-harness came unbuckled, and he fell headfirst. Both ankles were broken. He was hanging upside down when he was found. His head was in an anthill. He was unable to pull himself out.

After we cleared the first ridge of the Hump and were well into our mission, the cockpit started to fill with smoke. It smelled electrical, so we checked what we could. Both engines were doing fine, and the fuel and oil pumps were registering as they should, but smoke was still getting thicker in the cockpit. We were unable to find the source and thought it well to get out. The radio operator radioed to the nearest airfield at Chengkung, China, that we were about to bail out. The pilot was petrified. He was an old, non-military-trained pilot in his late twenties (I was 21). I was the co-pilot on that mission.

All three of us left the cockpit, got into our parachutes (checking the chest harnesses), and headed for the cargo door in the rear. We had put the airplane on automatic pilot.

We looked out a window in the cargo area and realized we would have to clear the stabilizer before pulling the rip cords on our chutes. If we didn't, we would be hit by the stabilizer, or our chutes could get entangled in it. It was a mighty big step out of that airplane. Besides, none of us liked ants. We decided to try one more time to get to the source of the fire.

We ran back into the cockpit, and that's when I noticed the source. An overhead panel containing lots of wires was burning. The radio operator grabbed the fire extinguisher and snuffed out the fire as I yanked the panel out. We called Chengkung to inform them we would be landing there instead of going on to Liuchow.

I am now convinced that an angel of the Lord had alerted us enough to the dangers of jumping and led us to try again to put out the fire and not take that Big Step.

CARPENTER OF NAZARETH

T HE HOLY SPIRIT REALLY got hold of me on March 23, 1973. I should have learned by that time to wait upon the Lord. But not me. I was so anxious to know the Lord, be part of the great movement of Christians that was sweeping through our lives, and receive the Baptism in the Holy Spirit that I heard about from others.

The late Rev. Deane Ballard came to Charlotte each month and held teaching sessions at several homes. Those of us who could, would sit with him to learn more about our Savior and the Holy Spirit.

On March 22, 1973, Deane held a Holy Spirit Seminar at Mouzon Methodist Church. After his teaching sessions were over, he invited those who would like to receive the Baptism in the Holy Spirit to stay a little longer. A small group of us gathered at the altar to pray. While praying, several people, including my wife Caroline, were being moved, being filled, and being joyfully surrendered to the power of the Holy Spirit. How happy they were.

But not me!

Why couldn't I feel this ecstasy? What was the matter with me? Lord, didn't You want me? I really felt left out and acted miserably. In fact, Caroline was so filled with the Holy Spirit and happy that I became jealous. I pouted. I was hard to live with the rest of that night.

The next morning, I grumpily went to my office at the Boy Scout headquarters. I told the receptionist that I was not in, and that I didn't want to see anyone or receive any calls. I closed the door to my office, cut off the lights, sat at my desk, and had a pity-party. I felt so sorry for myself that tears came to my eyes.

I mentally cried out to the Lord. And then the Holy Spirit spoke to me. Not audibly, but to my spirit. He told me to get a pen and paper and start writing. This is what appeared on the paper:

CARPENTER OF NAZARETH

Carpenter of Nazareth,
Are your hands so rough?
Or is my soul so evil
Uncaring and tough that
I don't feel your touch
Others tell me about?
Are your hands so rough?
Must I feel left out?

Carpenter of Nazareth,
Are you a vision or sight?
Or is my soul so blind
And full of fight that
I can not see your face
Others tell me about?
Are you a vision or a sight?
Must I feel left out?

Carpenter of Nazareth,
Can you speak or call?

Or is my soul so deaf
That I hear not at all?
Where is your soft voice?
Remove all my doubt!
Can you speak or call?
Must I be left out?

Carpenter of Nazareth,
You touch and you speak.
It is just my soul
That is, oh, so weak.
I reach for your hand,
I wait for your call.
I'm chasing you, Savior
-then I fall!

Carpenter of Nazareth,
With touch so sure,
Living today in
Hearts that endure.
Your voice is still heard,
From me you won't hide.
But I must remove
Self-pity and pride.

Carpenter of Nazareth
No vision at all,
Your touch is real
And I hear your call.
I need only to trust
In your Spirit in me

To feel the touch,
To hear and see
The Carpenter of Nazareth.

Twenty-six years later, I gave a copy of this poem to John Stafford, music director at Carmel Presbyterian Church in Charlotte. I asked if he thought it could be put to music. He said he would look it over. On May 23, 1999, John and the choir presented *Carpenter of Nazareth* as the anthem to the church congregation. I believe it was well received, to the glory of God.

I have had many lessons in self-pity since 1973. I received the Baptism in the Holy Spirit in 1974. But I must say that after I heard *Carpenter of Nazareth* set to beautiful music, my pity party was over. Thank you, John. Thank you, Lord. The *Carpenter* has come full circle for me.

SECOND CHANCE

F ROM THE TIME I was about eight, I have been interested in the world of creating things: carving, woodworking, painting, drawing, and other expressions of art.

At age eight, I entered a contest that was open to all the kids in Binghamton, Endicott, and Johnson City. The big bakery in the area wanted us to draw copies of *Skippy*, a popular cartoon character of that time. First prize was a red wagon, and I was very pleased that I didn't win it. Instead, I was really happy to win second prize - the biggest box of watercolors I had ever seen! Every color imaginable was in that big box. It meant more to me than any red wagon.

At age ten, I started carving balsa wood airplanes. You could buy an airplane kit for ten cents. It consisted of a block of balsa for the fuselage, a flat piece for the wings, two wooden wheels, some stick-on insignia, and a tube of glue. The instructions and diagram completed the kit. All you had to do was trace the shapes to the pieces of wood, carve out the fuselage, glue the other finished parts together, and you had a model airplane. Well, a little carving, shaping, sanding, painting, and so forth helped, too. I figured, if I could do all of the above, what I really wanted to do was fly the real thing. More about that in the section entitled *Now is Later*.

After joining the Boy Scouts, I did more carving. I made neckerchief slides out of wood, cow horn, and leather.

When I joined the Army Air Corps, the only carving I did was in India. I carved a miniature replica of the C-46 cargo airplanes we flew over The Hump. It was small enough to fit in a Robert Burns cigar box. After painting it, I added the number 1038 to the tail section. That was the number of the airplane on my first mission to China. Then I carried it with me on a mission, so now I have my model airplane at home that was on an actual combat mission.

After I was out of military service, I did more woodcarving and woodworking. I even took up oil painting and sketching.

But by the year 1973, I had a progressive hurting and pain in both wrists and hands. It was to the point where I could not use my hands to help lift myself from a chair. The pain and weakness seem to be totally engulfing my wrists and hands.

The reason I tell you about my carving, woodworking, painting, and drawing is to let you know how much I had the desire to create things. Part of this was also to gain recognition. I was even making some money creating things, but that was being jeopardized, and no one had an answer.

One night, May 5, 1973, our sharing group of six couples was meeting at the Castano home. We had been sharing and praising the Lord. Our praying was not in any formal pattern. We each prayed as we were moved and led by the Holy Spirit. The lights had been dimmed, and quiet hymns were playing in the background.

It was very late, and we had all been praying for quite a while. At a break in the prayer, even though I had been participating throughout the evening, I felt moved to ask the Lord to heal my wrists and hands. Nothing happened. I still had hurting wrists. Then, for some reason, it seemed appropriate to say, "Thank you, Jesus."

It was at that instant that I felt heat above my head. It traveled through my head, down my neck, across my shoulders, down my arms, and then into my wrists and hands.

Since that time, I have never had any hurting or pain in my wrists or hands except for some occasional arthritic discomfort in a couple of fingers in these latter years.

I was healed May 5, 1973. I was touched by my Lord, and that night I learned the only talents I have are the Lord's when He lets me use them. Every project since that night has started with a prayer for guidance, direction, and thanksgiving, as will all future ones.

All projects that are completed are accompanied by the following:

HOLY HACKINGS by a Christian Carver

You now own an original work of art designed and produced just for you. I do not claim any credit for the ability and talent required for its completion. Here is the reason, and truth, for this: Although I have sketched, drawn and painted for as long as I am able to remember, and carved wood, stone, metal and plastic, it was really for my pleasure. How I yearned to use my hands to create, a need to express myself, a desire for recognition.

For nearly a year prior to May 5, 1973, my wrists grew weaker and hurt more and more. It was difficult to lift myself from a chair with my hands and wrists.

My wrists were healed that night, thanks to JESUS CHRIST. Since then, I have asked the LORD to direct each project, and He has honored the request. HIS talents, expressed through me, have created this work of art, just for you.

PRAISE THE LORD!
R.W. Turner
July 7, 1973

That was the second time the Lord healed me. I cannot nor will not deny the power of the Holy Spirit in my life.

But God still had more lessons for me.

500 MPH Plus Straight Down

W HAT WE READ CAN sometimes resurface later. I'll give you an example. In 1944, I was stationed at the Army Airbase at Camp Davis, NC. I had been cleared to fly an SB2C, an A-25 dive bomber, which was used as a "target" for artillery and anti-aircraft students.

One afternoon, I climbed to 20,000 feet to experience the effects of anoxia (lack of oxygen) at high altitudes. I wanted to recognize the symptoms in case of a real emergency. I planned to remove my oxygen mask temporarily.

During my Aviation Cadet training, I volunteered to remove my mask in an altitude simulator so my classmates could see the effects of anoxia. It must have been interesting to the others, but all I remember was trying to write my name. My handwriting is bad in the best of circumstances, but you should have seen the scrawl that day. The next thing I remember was coming-to and the instructor holding my oxygen mask to my face. I had no after-effects, but it was a learning experience for me.

That afternoon in the A-25, I wanted first-hand experience. I knew that if I passed out, I would eventually come-to as I lost altitude. Sure enough, when I got to 20,000 feet, my eyes started to burn, and the instruments did not seem to be staying in place. Yes, it was just as it started to be in the altitude chamber months earlier.

I had to get oxygen fast. There was only one way to get it quickly. I did a split-S. This meant rolling the airplane upside down and pulling back on the stick.

The A-25 Helldiver is heavy. It redlined at 500 mph, telling the pilot it flies better with wings. If you exceed 500 mph, the wings might come off. So, the airplane is equipped with air brakes: perforated, extendable flaps. These help the pilot control his dive so he can better aim his bomb toward his target.

Because no one expected me to be dive bombing anything in that part of North Carolina, the person who certified me to fly this airplane never told me about the air brakes. Since the A-25 is a single-pilot airplane, no one was with me when I flew it for the first time.

The A-25 and I got oxygen really fast. But we were approaching the red line. So, I tried to pull back on the stick to come out of the dive.

Nothing happened.

I couldn't budge the stick. I put both hands on the stick and pulled.

Nothing happened.

Naturally, my feet were on the rudder pedals, so I practically stood up, and with all of my 125-pound strength, I still could not pull out of the dive.

Straight down we went. By now, the airspeed indicator had gone over the 500-mph mark. I expected the wings to fly away anytime.

Here I was, over the Marine Base at Camp Lejeune, NC, dive bombing those poor unknowing guys below, not with a bomb but some dummy in a dive bomber with no wings!

God's angels appear in all places. They even appear as resurfacing information from what had been read in flight magazines. My angel was in the form of an article I had read while waiting in the ready room at some airbase.

The article told about the pilots in P-38 fighters in England who were flying their airplanes straight into the ground. They would get into a dive and couldn't pull out before drilling a hole in the ground. The airflow over the surfaces of the wings was so strong that the pilot did not have enough strength to activate the control surfaces of the elevators.

Then someone remembered about trim tabs. These are little auxiliary elevators, ailerons, or rudder control surfaces on the corresponding main controls. They work according to Newton's third law of physics: for each action there is an equal and opposite reaction.

Therefore, if the hydraulically controlled trim tabs on the elevators were cranked or turned, their reaction would help the efforts of the pilot in pulling his airplane out of the dive.

Added to that, if you increase engine power gradually, you increase the effect of reaction on the main surfaces. Very simple. Provided you knew about that little life-saving tidbit.

My angel flashed that tidbit into my head. I trimmed the elevator a little. Then, I goosed the engine a little. Trimmed a bit. Goosed a bit. Trimmed a bit. Goosed a bit.

Pretty soon, I pulled out of that dive smooth as silk. No blackout at all. I was down below 5,000 feet in no time and had all the oxygen I needed. The Marine base was safe again, and I now know I was not flying solo. My angel was with me again.

As I look back, and I urge you to do the same, I see God has been taking care of me all along. I did not recognize it at the time, but at least I have learned that we gain many of our experiences and knowledge in order to be guided through the rest of our lives. Then, if we are smart, we will acknowledge that God has allowed these experiences so that one day we will turn to Him and thank Him.

Now is Later

I VAGUELY REMEMBER THE excitement when Charles Lindbergh flew non-stop solo from New York to Paris, France. I was five years old.

Perhaps because of all the talk about this brave young man, his goals, determination, and accomplishments, I claimed Charles Lindbergh as my hero. From then on, every time an airplane flew overhead, I was in it, in spirit.

How I wanted to fly! (I still look up when an airplane flies over.)

My first experience in an airplane came one evening when Mother and Dad took us three brothers to the Floyd Bennett airfield in Binghamton. It was located on the flats by the Chenango River. The runways were dirt.

Dad was taken up for a short flight in an old canvas and wood biplane. Mother refused to go for a ride, but Dad convinced her to allow us three boys to go up for one turn around the airport. Perhaps she thought that if we stayed in her sight, we would be safer. Knowing Mother, she prayed for us to safely make the flight.

My brother Hank, about twelve years old, sat on the left side of the front open cockpit that was designed to hold only one adult. My brother Roger, about seven, was in between Hank and me. I was about ten, sitting on the right side. All three of us sat on a bench seat and were strapped in with a canvas and leather belt. Being small, I could just see over the cowling of the cockpit. I doubt that Roger could see anything.

All I remember is the roar of the engine and the rather rough ride over the grass to the end of the runway. Being a tail-dragger, meaning there were two wheels under the lower wing and a skid under the tail section, we couldn't see anything until there was enough airspeed and the tail lifted. We roared down the runway, and suddenly we were in the air flying!

The wind in my face, the roar of the engine, the sound of air passing over the canvas wings and through the wood and wire struts and braces, even the odor of oil and gas, convinced me that I must become a pilot.

In the summer of 1942, I had already graduated from high school and had gone to work for IBM in Endicott. Because of the war, IBM was manufacturing gun parts. I worked on finishing the bolt-action for 20mm aircraft cannons.

Being on a swing shift allowed me to spend some days at a small airfield outside of town, where I took flying lessons for $7 an hour. I was just about to solo when I was called into the United States Army Air Corps on December 4, 1942.

I had qualified for entry into the Army Air Corps Aviation Cadet Program after I turned 18 in March 1942. In order to enlist as a pilot, you needed two years of college, but this requirement was waived because I was an Eagle Scout.

My status was upgraded to Aviation Cadet Candidate after a short time as an enlisted man in Atlantic City, NJ. Then I was sent to a College Training Detachment at Massachusetts State College in Amherst and finally shipped on a troop train to Nashville, TN, for classification.

Everything went well except I did not weigh enough to be a pilot. The medical officer authorized me to skip physical training, do no KP (kitchen police) duty, get all the milk I could drink, and go to the PX and drink beer every day for ten days. That was pretty tough duty!

There I sat waiting to get fat enough to hopefully ship out for pilot training with the next group. While all the other guys did KP duty, policed the grounds, ran, did pull-ups, push-ups, and all kinds of physical exercise, there I sat reading flight manuals, drinking extra milk, and swilling beer. I guess that's why I do not like beer to this day!

The day of reckoning came. I drank water, milk, and more beer. I didn't dare go to the latrine, so I swished over to the medical office and reported in, saying I had followed orders. The medic in charge got out my charts and records, took a look at me, and said, "OK, you qualify for pilot training." He did not even weigh me! But I am glad he didn't because I was already headed for the nearest latrine.

DIAMONDS ARE FOREVER

BECAUSE I WORKED FOR the American Red Cross as the Night Administrator, I was at home on the morning of May 30, 1979, when Caroline called, distressed. She had lost the large diamond from her engagement ring.

She was on her way out to the back parking lot of the American Red Cross, where she worked as an Administrative Assistant to the Public Relations Director. But first, she called to ask me if I would look around the house for the diamond while she searched her car and the parking lot. Have you ever noticed how asphalt sparkles in the sunshine, or how many tiny pieces of mica are embedded therein?

Where do you start a diamond search? I looked all around the kitchen floor and in a couple of rooms. Then I prayed. Getting a flashlight, hoping it would reflect the diamond as the light passed over it, seemed smart, but it was not until I got on my knees with the flashlight that, over in a corner of the kitchen, a bright reflection hit my eye. There was the diamond from Caroline's ring! When I called the Red Cross to get word to Caroline, there were lots of "Halleluiahs" and praises to the Lord.

Of course, you know the moral of the story. Get on your knees and ask for God's help. That seems to be a good start in any circumstance.

PASS IT ON

IN THE MID-70S, THERE was a 14-month peroid between jobs that turned out to be a very exciting time. For instance, our eldest child, Sharyn, was expecting her firstborn in Texas. Erik arrived August 1, 1974. Our youngest child, Nancy, married Jeff Blaylock on August 3, 1974. And my dad died October 3, 1974, in St. Petersburg, FL. We needed our luggage packed for all events.

Needless to say, there was a lot of leaning on the Lord. I was working in a commission-only position in a three-person personnel agency. This was during the height of the recession, when jobs were few and far between. Fortunately, Caroline was employed by the American Red Cross. I won't take space here to tell how the Lord provided for us, but He did give me the right leads to place clients and got us out of debt. Suffice it to say, I learned the lesson about tithing. Even though I made very few placements in the personnel agency, I always gave ten percent off the *top* of any commissions.

One evening, I was invited to go with four other men to some place in the hinterlands of South Carolina. To this day, I don't know where we went, how we got there, or how we got back.

We had been invited to give our testimonies to a group of farmers in a very small church. I don't think it seated more than 75 people. That night, there were approximately 30 people in attendance.

Each of us got up and witnessed how the Lord was manifesting Himself spiritually in our lives. My witness consisted of how we trusted the Lord to get us through the circumstances mentioned above. The emphasis was on trust and tithing. I'm not sure what else was said, but I guess the message was that the Lord always provides.

After we left the church, one of the men in our car surreptitiously handed me a folded piece of paper. He told me one of the farmers said he was convicted to pass it on to me. It was dark and I could not see what was in my hand.

Next, we went to a nearby hospital and visited a couple of people. It was in the hospital that I was able to see what was in my hand. It was a $100 bill. In 1974, that was a small fortune! God does provide!

I am not sure whether that gift was from a farmer or someone in our car who said it was from a farmer. The man who gave it to me said emphatically that it was from one of the people at the small church. I have always wondered how many farmers carry $100 bills!

I have also wondered if angels come in the form of farmers. Perhaps that was another angel in the church.

How that $100 bill helped back in 1974! It taught Caroline and me a lesson: when able, pass your blessings on to others. Since then, we have received the blessing of being able to pass anonymous gifts to others just as I received one that night, in the middle of nowhere, from someone who really cared. The blessing is in the giving.

BIG BOYS CRY - SOMETIMES

As LITTLE BOYS, I am sure we cried when we got hurt. Certainly, we cried when Mother or Dad, especially Dad, spanked us. But when we started school, we were taught that only girls cried. Boys were not supposed to cry because it was not manly or tough. It was just plain sissy. So, most of us managed to hold back the tears.

I believe I had not cried at all from then until January 3, 1945.

When WWII started, none of us brothers were in service. On the way to the World's Fair in New York City, our family heard Adolf Hitler give one of his memorable speeches on the car radio. My older brother Hank had invited his good friend, Heinz Rathmann, to go with us. His family had emigrated from Germany to the USA years earlier. Heinz spoke German and translated the speech that told us about the invasion of Poland by the Nazis. Hank was 17, I was 15, and Roger was 12. That was 1939, and we really did not think we would have to go into the military.

But by January 3, 1945, things had changed. Naturally, we had all grown older. Hank was in the Infantry and had received orders to report to New York City to ship out with his unit. He had been home on leave at this time for the holidays. I had gone through flight training, had become a Second Lt. Pilot in the United States Army Air Corps, and had received orders to report to Reno, NV, for transition training in C-46 airplanes.

Roger was now 17 and would be drafted in May or June of that year. Mother hung three blue stars in her window.

Caroline and I were married on October 8, 1944, and then transferred from Hinesville, GA, to Kansas City, KS. We left Kansas on December 22 to spend the holidays in my hometown before I would go on alone to Reno. What a trip that was!

Lt. Bill Lyman and his bride, Mary, a pilot in the WASP (Women's Air Service Pilots) program, were traveling with us. They were married about the same date as Caroline and I. Bill had received orders at the same time I had, and he and Mary were going to his hometown, Chicago, for the holidays.

The four of us left at 5 pm, with snow on the ground, but as we traveled further north, we ran into really icy conditions in Illinois. We were in a used 1940 two-door Pontiac that I had purchased in Hinesville.

Add to the four people in a two-door sedan all of the gifts that our families had shipped to us, not knowing that we were coming home for Christmas. The back seat and trunk were also full of all our earthly possessions.

We drove all night, taking turns. One of the fellows would drive with his bride beside him, and next to her was the other fellow, with his bride on his lap. Cozy but comfortable!

We let Bill and Mary out in South Chicago, where they caught a bus home. Caroline and I drove on to Ashtabula, OH. After skidding and slipping, we finally arrived at a hotel for the night. With a dinner of breaded veal chops and the rest of a hot meal, we had a good night's sleep.

Next morning we headed out again for Johnson City. My little Southern Belle got her first real picture of a northern winter landscape.

Once she said we were headed to "Oweege." I was really puzzled about such a place. It was not familiar to me. When I looked at the old map, I realized she had mistaken the spelling of Owego because the last "o" was on the fold.

Finally, after a long trip, we arrived in Johnson City on Christmas Eve in time to go to midnight services with my family.

A day or so after Christmas, Caroline went to see a doctor. It was confirmed that she was pregnant. I was awestruck, flabbergasted, fascinated, and otherwise on Cloud Nine. We were going to have a baby! But with all of this wonderment and happiness, it suddenly struck me. I had to leave the most precious people in my life: Caroline and our baby-to-be.

Arrangements were made for Roger and a friend to return Caroline and our Pontiac to Washington, DC, where she would meet her parents for the return trip to Wilmington.

Time to leave. Mother, Dad, Roger, Hank, Caroline, Baby-to-be, and I took a train to NYC, where Hank would meet a boat, and I would meet an airplane. He would go East, and I would go West.

That night, January 3, 1945, big boys did cry.

Mother and Dad cried. They were sending two sons off to war overseas, and their third son would soon be drafted.

I suspect Roger had tears in his eyes with his two brothers going overseas. That must have reminded him of his imminent future in service.

Hank wasn't much better off, leaving his parents, two brothers, a new sister-in-law, and a niece or nephew-to-be.

Caroline was in a strange part of the world with new parents-in-law, new brothers-in-law, and a newly announced baby-to-be, and she was saying goodbye to her husband of about three months. She cried.

Then there was the big boy who had not cried for years and years: me. Mother and Caroline were probably the only ones who had cried over the years. Yes, Mother and Dad were crying; Hank and Roger were crying; Caroline was crying; but this big boy led the way. I really showed them how to cry!

After the family got on the train and left, Hank and I went to a hotel to console each other. Mostly, Hank consoled me. That's what big brothers are for, right?

Somehow, we got through the ordeal, and we parted: Hank to his boat and me to my airplane. Reno was a heck of a place to send a new bridegroom! So, we all parted, and my big boy crying was over.

A TIME TO RELEASE

ONLY GOD KNOWS WHEN we are destined to leave our earthly bodies and go to be with Him in our new bodies in heaven. We who are left behind sometimes do not practice our faith, and we forget that God's timing must be fulfilled. Let me explain my thoughts, and at the same time admit that I have not always practiced what I am talking about in this section.

When a loved one is very ill and it seems he or she is suffering, or there seems to be no hope of recovery, or someone seems to be in a "vegetative state," I have a tendency to want to pray for divine healing, comfort, lessening of symptoms, and an easing of the stress that comes with protracted illness or aging. To me, there is nothing wrong with that.

But I have also learned that there is a time to release that person to be with the Lord. And in a way, I believe we contradict our faith by our selfish wishes to keep that person with us instead of "letting that person go" so they may be with the Lord. We need to release their soul and body to the Lord.

When I pray for healing or comfort now, I try to be sure to ask the Lord to show me His will and timing for the life of that person. In other words, I am presumptuous enough to tell the Lord that I release that person to Him according to His will. At the same time, I am comforted and put at ease by trying to practice the Lord's teachings.

This lesson was taught to me when Dad was suffering from a prolonged illness caused by a series of strokes. After the first stroke, he overcame paralysis, his speech returned to normal, and his handwriting was about as neat as usual. He even went back to playing golf. But the severity of his last strokes put him in the hospital for a longer stay, and he was eventually sent home, bedridden.

The last time I saw Dad alive, we were together in his bedroom. I had flown into St. Petersburg from Charlotte for a couple of days. Dad and I were able to talk about the Lord, and I know Dad is with Jesus. After Mother's death seven years later, I know that she is also with Jesus. The Lord led me to the joy of sharing my belief with my parents and hearing their story of belief and faith.

One morning, about 7:30 am, we received a phone call from Roger's wife, Jean. Dad had died during the night about 1:20 am on October 3, 1974.

My reaction? I praised the Lord!

Now this may seem odd that I could praise the Lord for Dad's death, but my spiritual growth had led me to realize that Dad had gone to his life, not death, with Jesus.

We can sometimes be an obstacle to our trust in God's perfect timing. For example, some time prior to Dad's death, I had prayed for his healing, comfort, and miraculous recovery. Instead, Dad got worse. His quality of life was not what he would have wanted. Perhaps my prayers were not in God's plans. Perhaps I was unwilling to accept the inevitable. Perhaps I selfishly wanted what may have been contrary to God's will.

On October 2, 1974, our Sharing Group was meeting at one of our homes. We had been in prayer for some time, and it was getting late. We had prayers of praise, supplication, direction, and healing well past midnight.

About ten minutes after 1:00 am on October 3, I felt moved to pray for Dad. I had asked for healing, but felt I needed to say I was willing to accept

God's will. I then asked for the faith and strength to let Dad be with the Lord and for me to accept the Lord's will. I released Dad to the Lord. Dad died about 10 minutes later.

Maybe my prayer was not what freed Dad to be with the Lord, but it freed me to accept God's will. That is why I was able to praise the Lord at that time. It was victory, celebration, and healing for Dad *and me*. In God's timing, Dad was truly healed, and I received spiritual healing too.

When Lightning Struck

STRUCK BY LIGHTNING! ON mission number 71, what proved to be my next-to-last mission, we were about to cross the "first ridge" on our return from China. Actually, it was the last ridge before we would let down toward the Assam Valley in India.

We were flying on instruments because we had entered a large storm. In those days, we had no Doppler radar or any way to detect the weather we were flying into. We were at approximately 16,000 feet, with 15,000-foot mountains below us.

Suddenly, a bolt of lightning, which looked to be the thickness of a huge arm, hit the left propeller hub, jumped across to the radio mast under our fuselage, and disappeared to our right.

Apparently, the lightning created enough charge in the air to cause the left engine to start failing. Or perhaps it changed the air pressure enough to interrupt the combustion in the engine and fuel mechanisms. I did not have time to analyze it. I just knew we needed that engine to keep running. We opened and closed the cowl flaps. We manually pumped the fuel pumps and changed the fuel mixture. We worked the throttles and did everything except jump out and turn the propeller. Actually, the propeller was still slowly "windmilling."

Somehow, the engine coughed and recovered. That was great news! But then the co-pilot exclaimed that the right engine had started to shut down.

Altitude was very important. We did not want to shear off the top of the mountains below. Suddenly, a great updraft put us at about 18,000 feet. Icing conditions would soon form. And we only had one engine, one that had already almost quit.

After much pushing of throttles, mixture controls, and using all the tricks we could think of, the right engine came back to life. Finally, we were in control of our airplane again, as far as the engines were concerned. But then we noticed that our radio was gone. Other vital navigation instruments were also gone. We had lost our radio directional compass and our ability to pick up directional radio beams back to our base in India. The lightning had melted our radio mast and some of the navigation system.

All we had left were our basic flight instruments: a ball-bank indicator, our barometric altimeter, and our magnetic compass. So where were we after being tossed about? We had to use what is known as dead-reckoning: common sense, intuition, timing, and flying by the seat-of-your-pants.

We flew in a south-westerly direction long enough to feel sure we were past the mountains. Still on those basic instruments in the clouds, we let down on a heading that we thought would put us somewhere in line with either our home base of Mohanbari or at least over flat ground. If necessary, we could belly-in on one of the great fields of tea in the Assam Valley.

To our great relief, we broke out of the clouds and saw the Brahmaputra River and other landmarks. This enabled us to change our heading to our home base, where we landed successfully.

Again, I don't think I consciously said, "Thank you, Lord." But I am now convinced the Lord had more for me to do, to grow spiritually, and to tell you that those angels over the Himalayas were still working on dying engines, lifting us over the mountains, and guiding our airplane to a safe landing.

THE CHAPLAIN'S JEEP

THOU SHALT NOT STEAL! Well, maybe just a little borrowing?

Our first child was expected on August 14, 1945. On that particular date, I was on a mission flying "The Hump" from the Assam Valley in Northeast India to a base in Western China.

Caroline was in Wilmington, halfway around the world. I figured I would write to her every day for a couple of weeks prior to the due date so she could have mail from me while she was in the hospital. Back in those pre-HMO days, the mother and new baby stayed in the hospital from 10 days to two weeks. Since babies don't come with instructions, they kept the mothers to give instructions, build confidence, and introduce this new state of motherhood.

As it turned out, after the two weeks of heavy letter writing, I figured I could go back to my usual routine of writing weekly.

To us, August 14 was memorable for two reasons. First, the war ended that day. Caroline went downtown to join in the big celebration, driving up and down Front Street with all the other happy people. Her mother did not think it wise for Caroline to be in heavy traffic at the time of the baby's due date because the excitement might start her into labor. But Caroline went anyway.

Second, the day was memorable because I didn't get any word of the arrival of our newborn.

I waited day after day. I was told "first babies can come even two weeks early" or "two weeks late." Also, "it takes time to get news to these out-of-the-way places, especially during a war." Although the war was officially over, we were still flying our missions into China, and our conditions had not changed.

So, I waited some more.

In the meantime, our daughter, Sharyn Elizabeth, finally arrived August 25.

My dad had sent a cablegram. Caroline's dad had also sent a cablegram. I waited.

My dad's cablegram never arrived, but the one from her dad finally arrived 10 days later, on September 4. In the meantime, Caroline had already received the deluge of letters from me.

It so happened I was on a mission to China on the actual day Sharyn arrived, so it was late that evening by the time I got back to my tent. When I walked into our tent, occupied by four pilots who called it "My Assam Home," I saw on my cot, under the mosquito netting, three things on my pillow: a bottle of whiskey (I did not drink alcoholic beverages and still don't), a little box of Robert Burns cigars (I did smoke but don't now), and a note saying there was a cablegram in the base post office (which was there then but probably isn't there now).

Great news! But what was the news? I realized the post office had closed a couple of hours earlier, but I trotted over to see if there was any chance someone was still there. There wasn't! Incidentally, the door was locked, too! I learned the post office was operated by the military personnel from Chabua, a USAAC base about 30 minutes from our base at Mohanbari.

Perhaps the Chaplain could help. So over to the Chaplain's tent I went, only to find he was gone for the evening. (Where does a Chaplain go at night in a remote part of India? Especially without his jeep?)

His jeep! If I couldn't get into the post office and the Chaplain was unavailable, perhaps I could get someone from Chabua to come back and get the cablegram out of the post office.

But I needed a jeep. I probably needed the Chaplain's permission to use his jeep. The Chaplain surely would give me permission under such circumstances, wouldn't he? This was an emergency, wasn't it? Besides, I could be back in a little over an hour.

Suddenly, I was in the jeep on my way that night, driving on the wrong side of the road (they do that in India). At Chabua, I could not find any post office personnel. So, I drove back to Mohanbari (on the wrong side of the road), parked the Chaplain's jeep that I'd "stolen," and returned to my tent. It was an excuse to open the bottle of whiskey, but I didn't. After all, hadn't I sinned enough by "stealing" the Chaplain's jeep?

The next morning, when the post office opened, I was first in line. Twenty-one days after her due date, I read the cablegram telling me I was the father of a beautiful little girl, Sharyn Elizabeth Turner. But I didn't set eyes on her until December 9, 1945, when I was back in the States.

Seeing Caroline and Sharyn that day erased all my frustrations and all the guilt about "stealing" the Chaplain's jeep.

THIRD CHANCE

My First Chance to follow God, my leg was lengthened. My Second Chance to follow God, my wrists were healed.

Not that I didn't try to be a better person after these experiences, I just didn't know how to surrender to my God. Something kept holding me back. God, Jesus, and the Holy Spirit were there all the time, but Dick Turner was missing something. That something wasn't supposed to make me a spiritual sage, or someone who shone with spirituality, or a modern-day Pharisee. What was missing was something called humility.

As I write these words, I almost feel that I am contradicting my lesson in humility that seemed to elude me, even after my other two chances. If humility taught me to focus on God and not myself, why should I presume anyone would want to read about my experiences?

My Third Chance was not only to see Caroline again, but also to humble myself by surrendering to Jesus: to get to know Him as a person, to listen to His direction through the Holy Spirit, and to share His message with you. Perhaps the desire to share how good God has been will eliminate the contradiction.

On December 29, 1997, I was diagnosed with prostate cancer. It apparently had manifested itself quickly because I had been faithful in having annual examinations. But there it was. For some reason, it did not seem to shake Caroline and me, probably because the doctor was so knowledgeable about the cancer and concerned for us.

I was scheduled to start hormone therapy February 13, 1998. However, on Monday, February 9, I was admitted to Presbyterian Hospital with pneumonia. I expected to stay there three or four days at the most for some intravenous antibiotics and rest.

On Wednesday, as Caroline and I were walking down the hospital hall with the mobile IV stand between us, suddenly my right leg felt like it had turned to stone. It did not tingle or feel numb. It felt heavy. It was as though I had one stone for a foot, another stone on top of that, and another on top of that. I do not remember walking back to my room, nor Caroline saying my right leg and foot had turned a deep purple, almost black. She called for the doctor.

I do not fully remember the events between February 12 and March 8. Some of the following comes from notes my family kept in a comprehensive log that our daughter Sharyn started.

On Thursday, the medical staff saw the condition of my leg and the results of the Doppler and ultrasound tests, and they called in a vascular surgeon. The surgeon ordered an arteriogram (also known as an angiogram) to provide a "roadmap" of the damage and location of the blood clots.

On Friday evening, the surgeon reported to the family that the clot was halfway up the thigh. The pictures showed the blockage worsened as it went down the leg, through the calf, ankle, foot, and toes. He said surgery may be an option, involving a femoral artery by-pass, but other options would be discussed Saturday morning, such as an occlusion coil procedure, and as a final option: amputation!

Amputation!

I seemed to surface from my "never, never land" when that one word was said. That word really got my attention, but then I was gone again. At some point, I apparently was hallucinating that I woke up in a hospital bed, and sitting on my chest was my bare foot. (Sometime later, the family kidded me about how I could have carved my own wooden leg and foot).

Saturday morning, the surgeon again outlined the various options and explained the Urokinase procedure that he favored. The following Monday morning, February 16, he started the first of these procedures, and my one day in ICU was extended to four. By Wednesday afternoon, the sheath was removed from my thigh, and a huge C-clamp applied pressure on the artery to prevent bleeding. I do remember telling the nurse that if they had let me know, I could have brought several C-clamps from my workshop at home.

I was then moved to a critical care area. My condition deteriorated to the point that I needed blood transfusions. It was apparent that I was bleeding somewhere.

On Saturday morning, another surgery was necessary to repair a "nick" in the artery. Caroline called our daughters. Our son, Rick, and his wife, Diane, stayed with Caroline, who was physically and emotionally exhausted.

Following this surgery, I was taken back to the ICU. The girls arrived later that day. When they saw Caroline's condition, they took over and made her go home to bed. The doctor confirmed on Monday, February 23, that she had the flu and needed rest. This was a particularly difficult time for both of us since Caroline could not come to the hospital, and I could not speak, even over the phone, due to extreme reflux and the removal of a blood clot from my esophagus.

On Monday, March 2, Critical Care Consultants were called in because my condition was worsening. They found pneumonia had recurred and that I was emaciated. They inserted a feeding tube in my nostrils to help me obtain the nutrition I was not getting. I had developed severe bedsores from weeks of being "scooted up in the bed," which eventually required a skin specialist.

On Thursday, as Caroline and family members went to get dinner across the street, she fell on the hospital sidewalk curb, broke her glasses, cut her face, and sprained her wrist. When she returned to the hospital the next afternoon, she was wearing a flexible wrist splint and a surgical mask, acquired from the nurse station, to hide the bruises and cuts on her face from me. Seeing her like this, I never felt so helpless, not being able to care for and comfort the love of my life.

That evening, I asked my daughter-in-love Diane to read to me the 139th Psalm. It is my favorite. Later in my recovery, I began to recognize the parallels of my experiences to this Psalm.

Apparently, my condition continued to worsen. A bone marrow diagnostic kit was placed on hold. Blood was ordered. A respirator was placed outside my room. And I had been unable to speak or hear for days on end.

A bit of humor never hurts. On Saturday, our close friends John and Peggy Garrett were sitting with me. I must have been pulling my oxygen mask off because it was very uncomfortable. The nurses told the Garretts I needed the oxygen in order to breathe. But I kept jerking the mask off, and John kept putting it back in place. Finally, he said, "Dick, you are at 20,000 feet in a B-17, and you need to keep your oxygen mask on!" Well, that did it! John said I grabbed the mask, slapped it on my face, and he had no problems after that.

As the days progressed, there was more bleeding, disorientation, inability to hear or speak, and the family put a "No Visitors" sign on the door. After about four weeks in the hospital, two surgeries, all kinds of tests, constantly being stuck by needles, being dropped to the floor by aids, having a sick and injured wife beyond my help, an oxygen mask to help me breathe, a feeding tube to give me nourishment, my legs and arms bloated with blood and fluids, a draining incision that needed changing every couple of hours, and a bottom I could not sit or lie on, apparently I was rather ill.

Sunday, March 8, seemed to be calm. Our minister, Steve, visited and later told me that I had asked him if I was dying. He told me he said, "No," but he later told Caroline that he really didn't think I would make it. Rick met Caroline and Nancy coming down the hall that morning. He told them not to try to communicate or do anything for me, but just to be there. He had written in large letters for me to read:

> This needs to be a day to *rest*, be calm, very little communicating with *us*, unless necessary, even when they put you in a chair. You must save your energy.

That Sunday evening, I became aware that I was in a place resembling an inward, tapering, black-walled area. At the end of this square-like tunnel was a white rectangle. Sitting in the center of that white rectangle appeared what I thought was Snoopy on a hospital bed. Most of us know the comic strip character Snoopy. He is a white dog outlined in black with floppy ears.

Suddenly, I was not looking at the white rectangle. I was *in* the rectangle looking outward, conscious that the black area was in front of me. Behind me, it was all beautiful and peacefully white.

It wasn't Snoopy on that bed. *I* was on that bed.

I knew it was me because of my hair. I had not had a haircut since early January, and I had plenty of hair on both sides of my head, but very little on the top. Lying on a pillow in a bed for weeks made my hair stand up on both sides, like Snoopy with his floppy ears.

I remember talking with God in my spirit. I said I knew I was very ill, and I was ready to go with Jesus. I was so uncomfortable, and I was tired of fighting. I just wanted it all to stop. Besides, it seemed so quiet, peaceful, and bright in the area behind me, and I did not want to go back into the black area.

But I had a favor to ask of God. I wanted to see Caroline one more time to explain to her why I was going away. I didn't want her to grieve for me, because I would be OK. I knew I had to tell her of my love for her one more time.

One of the lessons I've learned from this is that God is compassionate. He has a plan for everyone as to when they will die. But I believe that He honored my request and fit it into the framework of His plan for me so that I could learn more about Him and share with others.

Beginning March 8, I started to recover.

After a total of eight weeks in Presbyterian Hospital, I was transferred to Mercy Hospital for three more weeks of physical and occupational therapy. The therapists rebuilt all of my muscles from the waist down, getting me from the bed to a wheelchair to a walker. My goals were to walk again and drive an automobile. When I left Mercy Hospital, I was able to walk out, aided by a walker.

After further outpatient therapy for another eight weeks, I was discharged and was walking with a cane. Since then, I have returned to driving my automobile and walking without the cane. Praise the Lord!

It was several days after my Third Chance experience that the Holy Spirit revealed to me the meaning of the figure I had seen in the white rectangle. The figure was all white, with only a black outline. The white meant I was at the point of death. I had assumed that I was in a hospital bed, but there was no footboard or headboard. There was no furniture, not even an IV stand or machines. And I wasn't even wearing clothes. It was just me on a straight line.

Then it came to me! I didn't need to worry about clothing. I didn't need to worry about the headboard or footboard. I didn't need anything except that straight line that represented Jesus in my life.

When my time finally comes and I go into that beautiful white area, I won't need anything except my belief in God the Father, Jesus the Son, and the Holy Spirit.

That is why many people hear me say in a stressful situation: "straight line."

This *is* My Third Chance.

Angels in Israel

IT WAS OUR GOOD fortune to go on a tour of Israel on February 8, 1999. Many were skeptical about my being able to make the trip because of my illness one year earlier, but prayer is a tremendous enabler.

We flew from Charlotte to LaGuardia Field and then shuttled to JFK, where we boarded a 747 airplane for Tel Aviv.

One year to the day after I was hospitalized and received my Third Chance, I set foot in the Holy Land.

During the tour, we had wonderful experiences all over the country. There was a good bit of walking up and down pathways, through fields, on the shores of the Sea of Galilee, over the ancient ruins in Caesarea, Beit Sean, and Jerusalem. We put our feet in the headwaters of the Jordan River at Caesarea Philippi. We floated in the Dead Sea. We even climbed the last 88 steps up the cliff to the top of Masada. Sure, I had to use my cane to help steady myself. And the few times I had to handle my own luggage, someone was always there to help.

I believe that God uses ordinary people to act as angels, so we can learn one of His commandments: to help one another. Each time I happened to tilt a little too far backwards, I was amazed at how there was always a pretty little nurse named Sylvia behind me, giving me a slight push or touch. True, she was a member of our group, but how did she know I needed her at the right place at the right time so often? Even when Caroline and I were rededicating ourselves to God in the Jordan River, our pictures show Sylvia right behind me.

Other "angels" at various times were always there at the point of my need: Sherie, Rick, Sandy, and the two teenage boys, John and Brent, who helped me when I went for my "floating" experience in the Dead Sea and at the Jordan River, and especially Steve, my pastor.

Caroline experienced love and help from Margaret, Steve's wife. "Just a few more steps to the top," she would say to encourage Caroline. Margaret shepherded Caroline, and Steve shepherded me.

Why do I mention Sylvia, Margaret, Steve, and others? Because we prayed for God to give us strength, common sense, and good health to make this trip. And I know God answered those prayers. He used each of the many people on our tour as angels in Israel. I also believe many of you who read this will be able to look back and recount how you may have been helped by, or served as, one of God's "earthly angels."

Caroline and I were able to participate in the total tour of Israel because of the willing help of our fellow travelers. Don't be afraid to help others. It may be God using you as one of His angels here on earth.

Afterword

WHY DID I WRITE this narrative about my life?

My honest feeling is that this is not so much about my life as it is an appeal to anyone who will read these words. You may not have flown airplanes over The Hump. You may never have met an ex-convict. Not everyone has had the experience of being given words to a poem and then 26 years later hearing that poem put to beautiful music. But it is my belief that everyone has had an angel or two guide him, or even rescue him, at some time in his life. Some lives are a little less exciting on outward appearances, but all lives can be very exciting and fulfilling when a person begins to talk to the Lord and patiently waits for His reply.

It has taken me 75 years to recognize that when we open our hearts to Jesus and ask Him to lead our lives, He will do so. He will comfort us and provide for our needs. He will also give us the opportunity to be part of His fellowship, and He will give us the desire to share the great love that He has for us.

During the last 12 months, I realized that I should tell people God let me return from the edge of heaven to see Caroline one more time, and to give me another chance to know Him better. But I feel the most important reason is that I must learn to humble myself to the love that comes from my

Lord. I feel the need to urge others to share the wonderful joy that comes when one seeks, asks, listens, and obeys Him.

I share my hope that you will occasionally use your prayer time to surrender completely to the Lord in adoration and thanksgiving. When I did this, the Lord gave me a parting poem to share with you:

MY THANK YOU PRAYER

How many promises have I made
When I have prayed to you, my Lord?
Time after time I have sought your aid.
Does this strike a familiar chord?

I pray and I ask
I pray and I seek
But now you tell me
My prayer is too weak!

Oh what joy just filled my soul
As I prayed just thanking you!
I asked not, nor did I seek,
But thanked you all the way through.

Now I know how you want me to pray.
Don't just seek, but truly feel free
To thank you for your presence today
And the blessings you give to me.

You tell me to pray,
And right from the start
To thank you, O Lord

From deep in my heart.

Oh what joy just filled my soul
As I prayed just thanking you!
I asked not, nor did I seek,
But thanked you all the way through.

R. W. Turner
June 10, 1990

Perhaps my experiences in this book will help you recognize the chances the Lord may have given you in your life, as He has in mine, when I was given my Third Chance.

EXPERIENCING THE 139TH PSALM

S OME YEARS AGO, I started to write a novel about how our nation's blood supply was threatened by health service personnel using drugs. It was sort of an exposé in the form of a novel. The characters were formed, and the plot was developed. I was about to become a famous mystery writer. It never happened.

The Lord had other plans. New computerization, processing, and distribution eliminated all the possibilities for my well-crafted plot to ever happen. My story was way out of date. So much for me as an author.

Then came my Third Chance. The Holy Spirit has been nudging me to write, this time not for myself, but to share what He has done and is doing in my life. It started with the 139th Psalm, my favorite Psalm. On February 9, 1998, I was hospitalized in Charlotte, North Carolina, for a couple of days, which extended to eleven weeks in the hospital and eight weeks of physical and occupational therapy. During this time, my daughter-in-love Diane read Psalm 139 to me, and it came to me that I have personally experienced that Psalm.

On March 8, I almost went to be with my Lord (that is another testimony), but through prayer and love, I am able to be among you today to share my favorite Psalm. To me, my illness and recovery have an amazing parallel to the verses of Psalm 139.

Read the Psalm all the way through. Then read *Experiencing the 139th Psalm* all the way through. Afterwards, make a comparison verse-by-verse to understand *my* experience.

139 Lord, You have searched me and known me.
2 You know when I sit down and when I get up;
You understand my thoughts from far away.
3 You scrutinize my path and my lying down,
And are acquainted with all my ways.
4 Even before there is a word on my tongue,
Behold, Lord, You know it all.
5 You have encircled me behind and in front,
And placed Your hand upon me.
6 Such knowledge is too wonderful for me;
It is too high, I cannot comprehend it.

7 Where can I go from Your Spirit?
Or where can I flee from Your presence?
8 If I ascend to heaven, You are there;
If I make my bed in Sheol, behold, You are there.
9 If I take up the wings of the dawn,
If I dwell in the remotest part of the sea,
10 Even there Your hand will lead me,
And Your right hand will take hold of me.
11 If I say, "Surely the darkness will overwhelm me,
And the light around me will be night,"
12 Even darkness is not dark to You,
And the night is as bright as the day.
Darkness and light are alike to You.

13 *For You created my innermost parts;*

You wove me in my mother's womb.

14 *I will give thanks to You,*

because I am awesomely and wonderfully made;

Wonderful are Your works,

And my soul knows it very well.

15 *My frame was not hidden from You*

When I was made in secret,

And skillfully formed in the depths of the earth;

16 *Your eyes have seen my formless substance;*

And in Your book were written

All the days that were ordained for me,

When as yet there was not one of them.

17 *How precious also are Your thoughts for me, God!*

How vast is the sum of them!

18 *Were I to count them, they would outnumber the sand.*

When I awake, I am still with You.

19 *If only You would put the wicked to death, God;*

Leave me, you men of bloodshed.

20 *For they speak against You wickedly,*

And Your enemies take Your name in vain.

21 *Do I not hate those who hate You, Lord?*

And do I not loathe those who rise up against You?

22 *I hate them with the utmost hatred;*

They have become my enemies.

23 *Search me, God, and know my heart;*

Put me to the test and know my anxious thoughts;

24 *And see if there is any hurtful way in me,*
And lead me in the everlasting way.

EXPERIENCING THE 139TH PSALM

Perhaps if you read all of the following, you will feel as I do. Verses 1 and 2 should be the ending of my dissertation, but I start, knowing that God will give me only the right words and direction to share with you.

Verses 1-2: He has directed me through the past months of my illness and recovery, and, as long as I ask, hear and react to His directions, by believing that the Holy Spirit is my guide, He will bless my life no matter where I am. His knowledge of me and my thoughts will sustain me anywhere and anytime. He is with me always.

Verse 3: God, indeed, scrutinized my path and my lying down. A case of pneumonia put me in the hospital "for a couple of days" to get my fever down. That was on February 9, 1998. Indeed, the antibiotics did get the fever down, and I felt ready to get back home after about three days, impatient to get on with my normal activities.

On the 11th of February, Caroline and I walked down the hospital hall with the IV pole holding a bag of antibiotics. Suddenly, my right foot, calf, and leg to mid-thigh, felt like stone. Although I do not remember, we walked back to the room, and Caroline noted my lower right leg was bluish-purple and cold to the touch. My doctor was called; he scheduled an arteriogram. Then came the radiologists, hematologists, a surgeon, and an endocrinologist. God had me in the right place. Again, He scrutinized my path because blood clots were found in my right leg artery and the veins of both legs.

God knew I needed to learn the lessons of acceptance, patience, how to listen, how to be thankful, and He is working on my lack of humility. God knows my ways and my needs.

Verse 4: God is truth. I like to tease people, especially those close to me. Many times, my words come out, and people think I am serious. But I am learning that God knows what I am thinking and saying, so I make sure people know the truth, the jest, in other words, the humor of the tease, because words misunderstood, misleading, and unexplained can sometimes hurt. God knows the truth, so I must be careful not to leave untold the real truth of my words and statements just said in jest or tease.

Verse 5: How can anyone doubt the power of prayer! From the time we learned of my prostate cancer December 29, 1997, Caroline and I have been encased in an ever-growing cocoon of prayer, woven around us from homes in South Carolina, Texas, Florida, New York, New Jersey, Ohio, Georgia, and even as far away as Greece. Church groups have lifted up our needs, and we have heard from people that we don't even know. Especially when I was hospitalized and Caroline had a case of the flu and then fell, the cocoon of prayer and love grew and grew. We dare not get well! Blessed by God were those who prayed. Blessed are we who felt those prayers because God, indeed, placed His hand on us mightily.

Verse 6: When I recall where I have been, and how God gave His admonition to "pray for each other," I become very emotional and overwhelmed that I, even I, am a concern of others, as well as God.

Verse 7: I don't ever want to "go from Thy Spirit." Having almost been permanently in the presence of God, I can only praise Him for letting me experience His nearness, and wait for His decision when I will be truly in His presence forever.

Verses 8-10: God has allowed me to be in many places on this earth: from high mountains to flights across oceans, from places of great need to places of great affluence, from peaceful boyhood to places ravaged during World War II. While flying combat as a pilot in war, to the sweet experiences of marriage and family, in all of these times and places, I don't remember that I always sought God to direct my paths. But neither did I deny the existence of, and the need for, God's help and direction. I even prayed sometimes. Since our retirements, Caroline and I have traveled to many parts of the world, realizing that all of our blessings came from God. He was always with us, as near as our prayers.

Verses 11-12: This foundation of faith has convinced me that God has me in His light. Even my darkest moments are now lighted by His presence. God is everything good. Ask believing and be prepared for His light to show you the way as He has done for me.

Verses 13-14: After my illness, I appreciate the intricate "piece of clay" that I am. What wonders God created in man! "The foot bone is connected to the leg bone, etc," has real meaning after what the doctors did for my leg, indeed, my whole body. I hope those doctors realize they were guided by the Master Physician. My soul knows this truth well!

Verse 15: You made me, God. You put me together in your unfathomable creativity. You kept me alive to serve you, because

Verse 16: Only you know the number of my days. March 8, 1998, you allowed me to see myself about to be with Jesus. No fear, at peace, ready to see what was on the other side of darkness from where I was coming. I had no regrets. I, in my spirit communication, indicated I would like to see Caroline one more time to explain why I was leaving her. God knew how many days were ordained for me, but I now wonder if He granted me extra time, or whether He figured I was just not yet completed. I choose to believe He is a most compassionate God who has the power to make His plans for each of us, even perhaps a change or extension of time here on earth, fit into His overall plans for our eternal life.

Verse 17: Isn't God great to even think about such as me!

Verse 18: This is so great. I find myself more and more thanking and praising God for this, what I call "extra time." I keep wondering what I am to be used for.

Verse 19: I must not make the mistake of trying to interpret every circumstance as some "spiritual experience or leading." I must not let man's thoughts become hurtful or misleading to others. I seek only truth from the Holy Spirit.

Verses 20-22: My experience through this illness has put me in touch with my mortality, which is guided by the Holy Spirit. I must boldly but sensitively stand for truth, not accepting man's leading or those who speak against God. I believe my time on earth has been extended only as far as I am able to stand for my God, love my family and fellowmen who accept God's truth, and not allow the opposition to cloud my resolve to love my God.

Verse 23: It is hard for me to live as I know I should live because I live in man's world and am weak and frail. But I try, and I must keep on trying, to keep God in my thoughts more and more. I pray that God will enable me to better express my love and appreciation for this "extra chance", to praise Him, and to better serve Him.

Verse 24: I pray God will take away any hurtful ways in me as He did my physical hurtful ways during my eleven weeks of hospitalization, eight weeks of therapy, and who knows how long for recovery to what God has for me. God took away my "hurt." I must relate this hurt of a physical nature to the hurt I may have caused in many people over the years. I must humbly submit to the leading of God's Holy Spirit not to hurt others again. The more I can practice His presence in my life and can let God search me and know my heart, the more I can feel confident that God will lead me to everlasting life. Amen.

My hope for those of you who read this is that you will ask the Holy Spirit to lead you through the Psalms, applying them to your own life's experiences.

I dedicate this testimony to my wife Caroline, my family, and friends, and to all who sustained us through prayer, encouragement, and love. Praise the Lord!

Experiencing Deuteronomy Chapter 8

December 27, 1998

I HAVE USED MY favorite passage from Deuteronomy to show how to practice His presence in my life. Following is my testimony about Deuteronomy Chapter 8 that resulted from my hospitalization as described in *Third Chance*.

The scripture is from the *New American Standard Bible*, and I have divided it into four sections: a guide for the DIRECTION I must go; the RESULTS of my obedience; the CHALLENGE of God's plan for my life; and the ADMONITION of these verses that are not so negative as they are a promise and commitment for the fulfillment of my life with God.

I dedicate this to the love of my life, Caroline, and my appreciation for the efforts of my daughter, Sharyn, and all those who have been a part of the prayer cocoon that pulled me through this ordeal.

Read the following scripture all the way through. Then read Experiencing Deuteronomy Chapter 8 all the way through. Afterwards, make a comparison verse-by-verse to understand my experience.

1 All the commandments that I am commanding you today you shall be careful to do, that you may live and multiply, and go in and

possess the land which the Lord swore to give to your forefathers.
² And you shall remember all the way which the Lord your God has led you in the wilderness these forty years, that He might humble you, testing you to know what was in your heart, whether you would keep His commandments or not.
³ And He humbled you and let you be hungry, and fed you with manna which you did not know, nor did your fathers know, that He might make you understand that man does not live by bread alone, but man lives by everything that proceeds out of the mouth of the Lord.
⁴ Your clothing did not wear out on you, nor did your foot swell these forty years.
⁵ Thus you are to know in your heart that the Lord your God was disciplining you just as a man disciplines his son.
⁶ Therefore, you shall keep the commandments of the Lord your God, to walk in His ways and to fear Him.
⁷ For the Lord your God is bringing you into a good land, a land of brooks of water, of fountains and springs, flowing forth in valleys and hills;
⁸ a land of wheat and barley, of vines and fig trees and pomegranates, a land of olive oil and honey;
⁹ a land where you shall eat food without scarcity, in which you shall not lack anything; a land whose stones are iron, and out of whose hills you can dig copper.
¹⁰ When you have eaten and are satisfied, you shall bless the Lord your God for the good land which He has given you.
¹¹ Beware lest you forget the Lord your God by not keeping His commandments and His ordinances and His statutes which I am commanding you today;
¹² lest, when you have eaten and are satisfied, and have built good houses and lived in them,

13 and when your herds and your flocks multiply, and your silver and gold multiply, and all that you have multiplies,

14 then your heart becomes proud, and you forget the Lord your God who brought you out from the land of Egypt, out of the house of slavery.

15 He led you through the great and terrible wilderness, with its fiery serpents and scorpions and thirsty ground where there was no water; He brought water for you out of the rock of flint.

16 In the wilderness He fed you manna which your fathers did not know, that He might humble you and that he might test you, to do good for you in the end.

17 Otherwise, you may say in your heart, 'My power and the strength of my hand made me this wealth.'

18 But you shall remember the Lord your God, for it is He who is giving you power to make wealth, that He may confirm His covenant which He swore to your fathers, as it is this day.

19 And it shall come about if you ever forget the Lord your God, and go after other gods and serve them and worship them, I testify against you today that you shall surely perish.

20 Like the nations that the Lord makes to perish before you, so you shall perish; because you would not listen to the voice of the Lord your God.

EXPERIENCING DEUTERONOMY
CHAPTER 8

DIRECTION:

Verse 1: God's commandments, when kept, are the promises He made to fulfill my life. Trying to fulfill MY plans for MY life is doomed to fail until I follow HIS plans for my life. How do I know His plans? By keeping His commandments, seeking His direction, hearing His word, and following and obeying Him. This is done by prayer and being willing to listen. The Bible tells us God's plans, and all through the years, it has never changed. My 74 years should have been an ongoing obedience to that plan.

Verse 2: Looking back on my 74 years causes me to remember how God has led me through my "40-year wilderness." Whether I kept His commandments or not, He has tested me time and time again. Through His testing, He has humbled me over and over, and I haven't been smart enough to keep myself in the plan He has for my life. But God is faithful and has let me continue, because occasionally I may have done some of His calling by keeping His commandments.

Verse 3: I've never gone hungry, but hunger is not just for food or drink. God has humbled me by letting me hunger for a closer relationship with Him. He has provided me all my life with manna: His word, good parents, my precious wife and children, literature, and all kinds of spiritual opportunities. I didn't know what that manna was until I realized my "hunger and thirst" was not the satisfaction of bodily demands, but the satisfaction of my need for a closer relationship with him. His Word is my manna, which sustains me.

Verse 4: My clothing: all the good gifts of family, food, security, friends, and love, have not "worn out." Even though there have been times of distress and illness when, physically, my feet have swollen, all I need to do is look around me and see others worse off than I, and I thank the Lord that I am so blessed. Indeed, spiritually, my "feet have not swollen."

Verse 5: Fortunately, it has finally come to me that no good comes from blaming others for my shortcomings. It is I who has not asked God, listened for His answer, and obeyed His directions for my life. Without knowing it, I have been directed by my God, who has disciplined and revealed to me HIS plan for my life. When I wander off track, He straightens me out, and I again must obey His leanings.

Verse 6: So, God's commandments fulfill His promises when I walk in His ways and praise and revere Him.

RESULTS:

Verse 7: I am trying to fulfill His commandments and walk according to His teachings, but so often I fail. God is showing me the wonders of his creation. He meets all my needs daily. He allows me to live among His people, accepting their love and showing me how to return that love.

Verses 8-9: I may not have riches untold, vast lands and holdings, but I am rich beyond measure because I am getting to know God. I am alive and do not go hungry. I have opportunities to help others. But mostly, I have family and friends who know my God and are of like mind.

CHALLENGE:

Verse 10: Although I usually thank God for everything good when I pray, that is not enough! I think He wants me to bless Him by thanking Him for the little things in my life, such as open parking places, a good night's sleep, and even showing me how to work a knife on my carvings. So many times daily, He leads me toward His plan in my life.

Verses 11-14: The story of my life! Sure, I have thanked God many times for my many blessings. But too many times, I have kept moving on, thinking I was doing well. Many times, I seemed to get ahead, then hit a plateau. Sometimes I've been in the "doldrums of life." Then came the same question of how could I do better? How can I push harder to make ends meet? Where did I go wrong in order to not have more and more? Of course, the problem has always been the one simple word: "I." Pride in what I thought I had done, not being satisfied to wait on the Lord for what He had provided. Then came the times when again I realized that I had forgotten where all the good came from in my life.

Verses 15-16: My life, probably like yours, has been a mixture of rough times (like tight finances, illnesses, disappointments, loss of loved ones, broken promises) and good times (like tighter bonding of family, promotions, new life in the family, church friends). Family, friends, and church are the "water from the rock" and the "manna" in my life. The tests were from God, and so were the blessings.

Verse 17: Now there is no way that I can think in my heart that what I have and who I am can be the results of MY doing.

Verse 18: All the good that I have has come from God. If I am to realize any gains or any good, I must give credit to my Lord. He has promised this through the ages. I pray that my spiritual life and secular life will never fail to acknowledge this. I can only practice His presence daily, as best I can.

ADMONITION:

Verses 19-20: Oh, that I will never forget my God, never to put my thoughts and pride before my thanksgiving for what He does for me. Just looking around me (not in judgment but seeing consequences), seeing many not seeking God's direction in their lives, reminds me of where I have been. I pray not to return. God has tested me and continues to do so, keeping me humble, trying to get me to practice His presence as best I can, according to the depths that HE knows I am capable. This is my only way to eternal life with Him.

Amen.

ABOUT

RICHARD W. TURNER, SR.

*Lt. Richard W. Turner, US Army Air
Corps, 1944*

Richard W. Turner, Sr. (1924-2004) was a World War II veteran,
decorated pilot, artist, author, and devoted husband and father whose life
was marked by service, creativity, humility, and deep faith.

Born in Johnson City, New York, Turner answered the call of duty,
serving with distinction in the China-Burma-India (CBI) Theater. As a pilot,
he flew 72 1/2 missions over the treacherous Himalayan supply route known
as "The Hump", an experience that shaped his character and perspective
for the rest of his life.

After the war, Turner became a leader in the Boy Scouts of America, raised a family, was active in his church, and enjoyed painting, nature, and whittling woodcarvings. He shared 56 years with the love of his life, Caroline, and began writing in his later years to reflect on his life's most defining moments.

ALSO BY

RICHARD W. TURNER, SR.

Revelation ---at last

Revelation ---at last A heartfelt journey through love, loss, and eternal hope. In this intimate work, Turner reflects on the life he shared with his beloved wife Caroline and the emotional and spiritual path he walked since her passing. Through personal stories and scriptural reflections, he offers comfort and clarity on the promise of eternal life and reunion with those we love in Christ.

Stories from the Hump

Stories from The Hump A vivid and moving collection of wartime memories. The stories from Turner's service as a US Army Air Corps C-46 pilot flying over the Himalayas blend danger, humor, and the unseen hand of God. Turner captures the courage and faith of those brave airmen who flew The Hump in the China-Burma-India Theater of WWII.

www.ingramcontent.com/pod-product-compliance
Lightning Source LLC
Chambersburg PA
CBHW031443120626
46545CB00006B/2536